Some say……….

"The road to hell is paved with good intentions."

In regards to the history of The Preston School of Industry, that may very well be true.

Copyright © 2012
Cover Design: Sandra Montanez
Cover Photo Credit: Jay Silva
Back Cover Photo Credit: Roland Boulware

ISBN-13: 978-1481075046

ISBN-10: 1481075047

Published by J'aime Rubio, Author

All rights reserved. J'aime Rubio identified as the AUTHOR of the work in accordance with U.S. Copyright Act 1976 and all U.S. Copyright laws. No part of this publication may be reproduced, stored in a retrieval system, or transmitted in any form or by any means without prior written permission by the author/publisher. Some parts of this book have been previously published online via J'aime Rubio's blog "Dreaming Casually."

www.jaimerubiowriter.com

(Revised Edition)

Behind The Walls

A Historical Exposé of the Preston School of Industry

By J'aime Rubio

Acknowledgements:

I want to take the time to give a great big thank you to the Preston Castle Foundation, California State Archives, Scott Thomas Anderson, Amador County Library and Librarian Laura Einstadter, Kathryn Ramsey, Randolph Byrd, Tita Rodriguez Parra, Tim Ferry, Kevin Moore with the Oklahoma Department of Corrections, Roland Boulware & Jay Silva for their awesome photos of the castle, Sandra Montanez for her exceptional editing and cover design, to the various people interviewed regarding Anna Corbin's death who even after all these years still wished to remain anonymous, the former inmates who volunteered information to me and finally to all the tour guides including Eva Foreman and docents who spend much of their time devoted to restoring Preston to its former grandeur and teaching the public about its vast history. Thank you!!

This book is dedicated to the memory
of an invaluable piece of Amador County history,
Amador County Historian,
Mr. Larry Cenotto.

TABLE OF CONTENTS

Introduction		9
Chapter 1.	Founding of Preston	11
Chapter 2.	E.M. Preston & E. Carl Bank	14
Chapter 3.	Attempting to Avoid Scandal	18
Chapter 4.	How Ione Boys Were Tortured	21
Chapter 5.	The Escape Artist	27
Chapter 6.	The Murder of Joseph Morgan	33
Chapter 7.	Herman Huber's Death & Fake Escapes	37
Chapter 8.	The Death of Sam Goins	42
Chapter 9.	Infiltrating the Castle	48
Chapter 10.	The Cemetery—The Boys Buried at Preston	55
Chapter 11.	Who Killed Anna Corbin?	60
Chapter 12.	A Senseless Death of the Agricultural Teacher	78
Chapter 13.	Famous and Infamous Former Wards	79
Chapter 14.	Final Thoughts	83
Bibliography		87

PRESTON CASTLE

Introduction

It stands atop red clay mounds, almost like a palace sitting on a mountain top. It's Gothic and Neo-Romanesque Architecture is one that creates a dark ambience for all who gaze upon its archaic exterior. Preston Castle, located in Ione, is one of California's most historical and beautifully constructed buildings. It is also a place full of dark and tragic stories that many people are not aware of. Over the years, many people have taken an interest in learning about the history of Preston, but only some of the more popular stories have lived on, while many other stories have been long forgotten and left unspoken.

I have lived in Amador County at different times in my life and can honestly say that I have always been drawn to Preston Castle. In the past four years I have been researching, collecting and documenting many stories, some known and some unknown to the public. It has been a labor of love in order to shed light on Preston's vast history. It wasn't until a few months ago that I finally decided to put all of the stories together into a book. That way, other history lovers can finally read about Preston's secrets.

What you will find within this book may surprise you, and yet there are so many different tales still left untold. Unfortunately, I have only scratched the surface, revealing just some of the many horrific and mysterious accounts at the infamous Preston School of Industry. I hope whoever reads this book sees the effort I took to compile all of these stories together in a book form. I will never truly be finished researching and investigating the hidden secrets buried deep within those ominous brick walls. Perhaps later on, I may write another book adding to the many stories I have still yet to uncover.

Sketch by Joaquin Miller, San Francisco Call

CHAPTER 1.

Founding of Preston

Long before California was a part of the United States, the land we know today as Ione was first inhabited by the native people known as the Miwok Tribe. At one point the Spanish, although continuing to allow the natives to live on the land, claimed this area as their own, thus initially making it part of Mexico's territory. In fact, the very site of Preston Castle is built on the land that once housed a Miwok Village.

In 1890, the State reached an agreement with Ione Coal and Iron Company to purchase 330 acres of the Rancho Arroyo Seco, (meaning: "Dry River Ranch") part of the Mexican Land Grant for $20 per acre.

According to *"The Preston School of Industry: A Centennial History 1894-1994,"* by John F. Lafferty, it states that the state acquired 230 acres of land at $30 per acre (with 100 acres donated). It also states that 250 acres of land across the road was also offered to the state as well.

Once the state acquired the land, then they needed a water source. Being that Ione didn't have adequate water at the time, the owners of the Henderson Ranch made an offer they couldn't refuse. Michael and Bernhard Isaacs told the State that they would give them rights to 750 inches off the creek named "Sutter Creek" that ran through their land. Once land and water sources were set they began their planning for building of the Preston School of Industry.

In December of 1890, the laying of the cornerstone and time capsule was presided over by E.M. Preston acting as the Grand Lodge Master of the Masonic Lodge. Building of the "Castle" commenced thereafter. By July of 1891, the project had run out of funds and had to borrow $25,000 and appropriate nearly $170,000 in order to pay off their loan, furnish the entire property, purchase all the machinery and supplies for the Industrial School and also finish the building of the entire school.

The Romanesque Revival (or Neo-Romanesque) design was created by architect, Henry A. Schultz (sometimes spelled Schulze). Preston was just one of many buildings designed by Schultz. He also designed the James A. Folger House in San Francisco and also the Kern County Land Company in Bakersfield.

The very sandstone to make the bricks used on the "Castle" was quarried just a few miles down the road. The prisoners at San Quentin labored over the brick making process. The bricks then travelled on railcars back to Ione to be placed into the very structure that stands today. Upon the completion of the school, an article written by famous writer, Joaquin Miller, for the San Francisco Call compared the school's stonework to that of the Spreckels' Palace, that once stood on the corner of Van Ness and Clay Streets, in San Francisco.

This is a current view from looking out of one of the turrets of Preston Castle.

This was the Infirmary at Preston where many of the boys were treated.

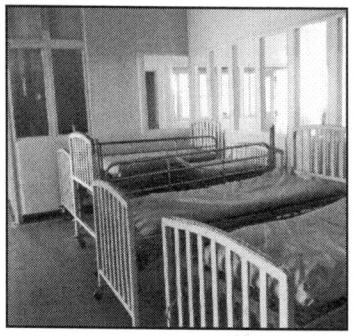

Imagine yourself here in the room which was used as the library of Preston.

- 13 -

CHAPTER 2.

Edward Myers Preston & E. Carl Bank

When you think of Preston Castle, you have to think of the man the school was named after, Edward Myers Preston. But who was this man, E. M. Preston?

Edward Myers Preston was born around 1842 in Michigan. He later lived in Nevada City and worked as a banker. As a Grand Master Mason he presided over the Masonic Grand Lodge. He was also a very political man, becoming a State Senator. On January 29, 1889, he introduced the Senate Bill No. 402, establishing a state reform school at Folsom after E. Carl Bank approached him with the idea. Originally, Preston was meant to be built in Folsom, however, Ione proved to be a better choice. At a later date, Senator Anthony Caminetti of Amador County, reintroduced E.M. Preston's bill establishing "The Preston School of Industry" at Ione.

On March 11, 1889, Governor Robert Waterman signed the amended bill into law along with contracts to start construction on the Castle began.

The Preston School of Industry was named after E. M. Preston, who lived only a few short years after the school opened. He died on April 24, 1903 in Nevada City, CA. He is buried at the Pine Grove Cemetery with his wife Maggie Preston and their daughter, who died in infancy, in Pine Grove Cemetery, Nevada City, CA.

Who Was E. Carl Bank?

E. Carl Bank was the very first Superintendent of the Preston School of Industry. In fact, after learning about his role in how Preston started, some may feel that The Preston School of Industry should have been named after E. Carl Bank instead of Edward. M. Preston. The San Francisco Call stated that Bank was the one who begged the state for the opportunity to have minor boys come to this new reform school. However, it was Edward M. Preston, President of the Board of Trustees who "got the ball rolling" by introducing the Senate bill that made idea for the school possible. Thus, it was Preston himself, who started the school.

The Preston School of Industry was created for the purpose of giving minor boys a stepping stone in life that they would have not acquired had they stayed at San Quentin. It was to be a place where wayward boys would have the ability to earn a decent education, self discipline and a trade in order to make a living and flourish when they were released out into the world.

The school was set up in three departments:

- Academic
- Military
- Industrial

E. Carl Bank was appointed Superintendent by the Board of Trustees, E.M. Preston, Adam Andrew and Fayette Mace. Bank took office as Superintendent as of November 11, 1893 before the school technically "opened."

According to the newspapers, the idea was brought to the State to allow the opportunity to start an "annex" or subsidiary institution for minor boys who needed help, not punishment. You see, in the beginning, not all of the boys at Preston were criminals. Actually, most were mainly orphans, abandoned or just plain homeless. The ones who were considered criminals were generally because of petty theft and truancy due to the fact of being homeless in the first place.

During that time period, there was no place for incorrigible, truant or just ill behaved boys. Neither was there a place for orphaned or homeless young boys between the ages of 8-18. The only option the State had at the time was to ship all boys, no matter what their circumstances, to San Quentin Prison. It was reported that Bank took a fondness to the boys he moved to Preston when it opened. He considered them his "little companions" and took them with him all over town. His wife also took a liking to the youngsters and they considered them part of the Bank family.

Superintendent Bank seemed to be truly dedicated to help steer young boys and young men to become good members of society, not by punishment or harsh treatment but with love, kindness and wisdom. He knew that if he could help these boys during the few years he would have them that they could receive the best education, self discipline from military training and last but not least, they could learn a trade.

By giving them the best chance possible, he then could set them out into the world with a fighting chance to be successful in life as adults. Sadly, this would not last for long.

The Preston School of Industry opened its doors to the first wards on June 13, 1894. The school officially opened on July 1, 1894. The first seven wards at Preston were (as seen in photo): James Carner, Alexander Cassulo, Alfred Jacobs, Walter Kavanaugh, James O'Donnell, James Phillips and Burt Starr.

First seven wards at Preston - 1894

CHAPTER 3.

Attempting to Avoid Scandal

In April of 1895, Superintendent Bank was thrust into a scandalous light by four employees, or rather, former employees of the school. Herbert S. Martin, Matthew Bridge, C.H. Brown and W.F. Eastman brought allegations to the San Francisco *Examiner*, stating heinous accusations on the part of Superintendent Bank.

In the book, *"The Shurtleff and Lawton Families- Genealogy and History"* by William and Lawton Shurtleff, it states that Herbert Martin had made the allegations against Superintendent Bank as an act of courage in order to bring forth the wrongdoing that was taking place. It goes on to quote from the San Francisco Examiner that the *"boys were ill treated, overworked and insufficiently fed."*

Notations elaborate that the school rooms were overcrowded for months. In upwards to 33-50 boys were cramped into the classrooms, while windows were sealed shut, leaving unhealthy and musty air for the boys to breathe. According to Martin, there wasn't enough bedding, pillows, blankets or even books for the boys. Claims were made that Superintendent Bank disregarded the Board's orders to implement military work into the boys' schedule, and instead overworking the boys on hard labor jobs.

Accusations continued that Bank was not only neglectful to the boys' welfare, but also physically abusive to boys, whipping them until blood ran from their wounds and even dragging two handcuffed boys before a horse as a form of punishment.

The accusations didn't stop there. It was said that officers and wards were fed sour bread and dirty water. According to Martin's statement, the sewerage from Sutter Creek ran off into the creek that fed Preston's water supply leaving the water filthy and unfit to drink.

Another former employee, Mr. Bridges stated, *"In rainy weather, the boys, some 170 in number, now are all huddled together in the dark basement on a concrete floor with no occupation on any sort provided."*

Mr. McLean, the gardener also commented that some of the boys sent to work with him outside were fainting from lack of food. He even refused to take on any wards to work for him unless Superintendent Bank made sure they were properly fed beforehand.

According to W.F. Eastman, the electrical engineer and another one of the accusers, he stated that *"The Superintendent gets $175, his house rent and his family supplies. Besides, he gets all this servants from among the boys. He has a dining room boy, a kitchen boy and any other boy he wants. He is an autocratic officer and has won the title of "Little Czar On The Hill."*

A highly politicized investigation was started by the "Legislature Committee," lasting only a couple of days long. Citizens of Ione held an "indignation meeting" to support Superintendent Bank. The allegations brought on by the four former employees were denounced as being "untrue" and further statements claimed that accusers were the ones committing wrong doing.

According to the businessmen who spoke at the meeting, the four men who had been "dismissed" from their duties at the Preston School had been rightfully removed for bringing discredit to the school by being seen in town drinking at bars while in uniform.

Martin, Bridges, Eastman and Brown had been paid quite well for their positions. It was stated that this fact did not stop them from complaining about their work load. It seemed that it wasn't until the four had been dismissed from their duties that they brought on these accusations against Bank, making it their word against his, and leaving many to doubt who was actually telling the truth.

It was stated that Preston Senior Librarian, John Lafferty, had mentioned that perhaps Martin's story was true, but being that the town of Ione was so dependent on the school during that time period, there was little to nothing that could be done. All accusations were dismissed against Superintendent Bank and the school continued to function without reproach.

Chapter 4.

How The Boys Were Tortured

On May 20, 1897, E. Carl Bank was removed as Superintendent purely for *"Political Reasons."* The media stated that there was never any proof of real misconduct by Bank and that he was a loyal and faithful Superintendent to the institution. E.M. Preston voted against the displacement of Bank but the other two Trustees voted him out 2 to 1. The man to replace Bank was none other than Dr. E.S. O'Brien, a Democrat from Merced. Preston's very words were quoted saying, *"This is the first time politics has entered into the management of the school.....I regard it as unfortunate for the school and for the State. I do not know that the newly appointed Superintendent has had any experience in the management of reformatory institutions. I think that question was not considered."*

The plain and simple fact for O'Brien moving into the position of Superintendent was because he "wanted it." This was due to the fact he knew people in high places. Because of his political ties, he was able to boot E. Carl Bank out of the very position he had created.

Dr. E.S. O'Brien's reign was the start of a terrible legacy that was rumored to have lasted throughout many decades even after he had been long gone. That legacy was cruelty. From the very beginning of his days at Preston, O'Brien ruled over the boys with an iron fist, literally. Rumors and gossip spread around town of his terrible temper and lack of self-restraint. By November of 1897, O'Brien had earned the title of "Tyrant." Seven people which included employees and wards, filed petitions and affidavits with the Governor accusing O'Brien of *"awful brutality"* and *"torturing the wards."*

H.R. Bernard, the Board Secretary for Preston stated this about O'Brien, *"He who cannot govern himself, must not expect to govern others."* Bernard went on to accuse O'Brien for mismanaging the school and having an *"uncontrollable temper."* He also claimed that O'Brien's *"egotism persuaded himself that he is indispensable and harbors under the hallucination that, as he expressed it, he is a 'stone wall' and 'cannot be removed'."*

Bernard continued to state an account that would then be the start of many stories to come, which inevitably earned the school the title *"Preston School of Scandal."*

ACCOUNT:

" I was called upon one evening to report immediately to the Superintendent's office, and rushed in to find Dr. O'Brien wildly excited and beating A. Ascensio over the head and face with a cane, which he soon broke. He continued his blows with the part left in his hand which was also broken a moment later from the force of the blows.

Then the Doctor grabbed a pole about four feet long and proceeded to belabor the yelling lad over the body. The force of the blows was terrific.

I have also witnessed a rough and tumble fight on the front portico of the administration building between O'Brien and a 16 year old lad from Ione…. Each pummeled the other for some time, until a blow from O'Brien cut the lad's face. The boy was allowed to go, but later Mr. Phillips, an officer of the school and Deputy Sherriff, was sent after the boy whom he brought back and was taken to the Superintendent….. O'Brien became brave and threatened the boy that if he ever dared to speak to him in Ione that he

{O'Brien}, who had just handed the revolver to Phillips, would blow a hole in him that a team could run through"- H.R. Bernard's Affidavit.

Another account was recorded by Amador County Physician, E.E. Endicott on 11/14/1897, reads:

"This incident, among many others of a similar nature, came under my personal observation while in professional attendance at the said school, and serves to confirm in my mind, as I believe the of many citizens of Ione, the serious charges now appearing in the daily press...

A youth by the name of Nick Hamilton, in an endeavor to escape, had sustained a sprained knee. When called in to attend the injured lad I found him lying in the hospital suffering great pain. I examined the knee and found it badly swollen and inflamed. Dr. A.L. Adams of Ione had also examined him and confirmed diagnosis. Treatment was at once instituted with a view to relieving the suffering boy, when the Superintendent appeared and desired to examine the injury.

He rudely grasped the boy's limb, and to our astonishment began vigorously flexing, extending and rotating the limb, heedless of the yells of pain emanating from the tortured boy, his only reply being "Lie Still, I'm Boss Here!!"- E.E. Endicott, M.D.'s Affidavit.

One note I would like to make right here is that this boy, Nick Hamilton, died six months after this story was published in the paper. His cause of death according to the Biennial Report states he died from "pulmonary tuberculosis" and that he was kept "isolated" from all the boys.

Maybe the poor boy didn't survive O'Brien's torture, so they made an excuse that he died from tuberculosis. His body was never claimed so he was laid to rest in the cemetery behind Preston.

Superintendent O'Brien seemed to be cornered now. Not only had the Board of Trustee's Secretary and the local Physician made accusations in regards to O'Brien's tyrannical abuse, two more witnesses P.J. Glas and J.J. Harlon stated that O'Brien "flogged a boy until his flesh peeled from his back." He also "lashed" another boy until he "exhausted him to the ground."

Sadly, although so many came forward to testify against O'Brien for his misconduct and vicious cruelty to the boys, he was exonerated. According to the December 18th edition of the 1897 newspapers, the headline read *"Dr. O'Brien Has Been Vindicated."* It was obvious there was some sort of payoff and cover up on the part of O'Brien and his friends in high places. Even the Governor himself couldn't seem to have anything done to O'Brien despite his very best efforts.

In regards to the entire investigation, The Board of Trustees for Preston ruled in favor of O'Brien, completely exonerating him of the charges of cruelty and unnecessary severity to inmates. The vote passed 2 to 1, being that Trustee Tyrrell voted negatively towards O'Brien. Unfortunately, O'Brien got off without so much as a slap on the wrist and even threatened to sue the State if they alleged any more wrongdoing. He was asked to resign on good terms to avoid any further scandal and he agreed as part of the stipulations of his investigation.

After O'Brien left, then entered David Hirshberg, the newly appointed Superintendent of the Preston School of Industry. The scandals and stories of terror and torture at Preston had just arose to the surface and more would soon come.

By January of 1898, The Preston School of Industry had seen two Superintendents come and go. Now there was a third, David Hirshberg. Along with Timothy Lee, appointed as Assistant Superintendent, Hirshberg took on the role as quickly as possible. Hirshberg's newly appointed reign would not be without its share of scandals for that time.

Remember, the majority of boys at Preston were not hard core criminals. Actually, many of them were sent there for things such as vagrancy, disturbing the peace, incorrigibility, even vulgar language. Others were orphaned or abandoned at a young age where they learned the "hard knock life" and ended up at Preston for things such as burglary, larceny, and assault.

FROM OPENING OF PRESTON 1894 TO 1898

Wards Incarcerated For:

98-Burglary
6-Malicious Mischief
32-Grand Larceny
4-Assault
87-Larceny
3-Battery
81-Vagrancy (Homeless)
2-Indecent Assault
5-Forgery
1-Vulgar Language
4-Misdemeanor
2-Incorrigibility
4-Attempted Rape
2-Infamous Crime
1-Indecent Exposure
5-Embezzlement
2-Disturbing the Peace
1-Robbery
2-Felony
1-Arson
2-Assault with a Deadly Weapon

CHAPTER 5.

The Escape Artist

The story of former Preston ward, Robert E. Byrd started long before his stay at the Preston School of Industry. In fact, to understand why he ended up there at all, one would need to know his back story.

Robert E. Byrd was born on January 8, 1882 to parents Joseph Edgar Byrd and Helen M. Wilder. His father, Joseph, was a Confederate Veteran from New Orleans, LA, while his mother Helen had been brought up the daughter of a farmer and former Union Soldier from Forestville, New York.

As certain as the tales of Romeo and Juliet, it was also obvious that the pair were in love. They even went so far as running away together against Helen's father's wishes, later eloping in Covington, Kentucky. Helen's father did not approve of her marrying a "reb," as Joseph was from the South while Helen's family was from the North.

After marrying his love, Joseph became a traveling salesman, who represented cotton brokers, publishers and dry goods suppliers to retail stores, while Helen became a seamstress to make ends meet. They traveled a lot during their first years of marriage, going from Louisville, KY, Evansville, IN, and Nashville TN.

In 1881, due to the tiresome life of being a traveling salesman with a family, Edgar Byrd chose to become an entrepreneur by opening a tavern in Florence, AL, hoping to make roots there. Unfortunately, this choice proved more harmful that good. In late December, Edgar Byrd became entangled in a fight with the former Mayor of Florence inside of his own tavern. The fight broke out and took to the street where it ended in a shootout, leaving the former Mayor dead. Although Edgar was indicted for murder, the charges were later dismissed due to "self defense." After being subjected to extreme stress, Helen gave birth to Robert two weeks later. Eventually, the family sold the bar and moved their family elsewhere.

Around 1884, while traveling for work, Robert's father, all alone in his hotel room, died from malaria. Suddenly, Helen became the sole provider for her children which must have put a strain on her. She eventually moved back to her home county of Chautauqua County, NY. Once there, she bounced from boarding house to rented houses for many years, never being able to give her children the sense of stability she yearned for. After the death of her youngest son William, Robert seemed to have strayed down a path of delinquency. This was more than likely due to the lack of a father figure, unending hurt from the loss of his father and brother and also instability at home.

By the time Robert was 12 years old, he had been in trouble with the law. In 1894, he was sent to the Burnham Industrial School in Eastern New York State (now the Berkshire Farm School) where wayward boys were taught to farm. He received a rigorous education there, until his release on March 1, 1896. He then when home to Fredonia, NY, only to get arrested again three weeks later. By March 26, he was sentenced to the New York Industrial School near Rochester, N.Y. For two years he served his time in a manufacturing trade school environment not so different from Preston. By January of 1898, he was paroled into his mother's care, moving to Buffalo, N.Y.

**Cadet Robert E. Byrd-
Circa 1898**

TWO YOUNG DESPERADOES BAGGED BY THE OFFICERS

They Are Wanted at Irvington, Oakland and Other Places For Many Crimes.

Two slick young chaps drove up to the Irvington Hotel at Irvington on Thursday evening and stated that they wished to put up their horse and stay over night. They were accomodated and in the morning made complaint to Mrs. Haight of the hotel, that they had been robbed of $90 and a gold watch during the night. They were closely questioned and on this disclosed out on a charge of grand larceny, and an effort will be made to land these two young sharpers behind the bars.— Press.

Jesse Russell, one of the above men wanted, was arrested last evening by Sheriff Langford and Deputy [...] Russell has been sent [...] days at a prison [...]

As the Byrd family story goes, while Robert was working as a clerk in Buffalo, he became restless. He then ran away to California at the young age of 17.

Apparently, due to the stories of endless opportunities out west along with the romanticized folklore of the "get rich quick" life during the gold rush, he travelled to the Golden State with dreams of making it big.

News accounts of that time period even mentioned that Robert went west "on a wheel," meaning he rode his bicycle from New York all the way to California. By the fall of that same year, Robert had made it to Gardnerville, Nevada and then onto Reno. After finding himself in trouble once again, Robert sold his bicycle and bought a train ticket to San Francisco.

How Robert E. Byrd Ended Up In Preston

In November of 1899, Robert had made friends with a piano player, Jesse Russell. Eventually the two teamed up and decided to steal a horse and buggy rig in Oakland. Driving the buggy to Irvington, they stopped to stay at the Irvington Hotel and skipped out on their bill. Leaving the horse and buggy behind, they left on foot onto San Jose down the railroad tracks, more than likely hitching a ride on the train as it rolled by.

By the time Robert had made it to San Jose, he stole another horse, this time taking it from a livery. He had played the part of a potential buyer wanting take it for a trial ride with the full intention on purchasing it, however he never returned. He rode that horse all the way to Solano, CA. He was then apprehended on November 16, 1899, being charged and tried for Grand Larceny in January of 1900 and sent to Preston for three years.

Within two months of being sent to Preston, Byrd had become an 'escape artist', walking out of Preston undetected. He did so by making a false key and opening his way out of the building. Within three days he was captured. Once again in July he attempted to escape only to be caught again.

By December, it was reported that Byrd had broken into an officer's room and stolen his revolver, concealing it for weeks while the officer never noticed his gun was gone. I don't know about you, but one would think that as an officer at a boy's youth reformatory, how could you not know that your gun was missing for weeks?

That information from the officer makes me think the gun was actually planted in Byrd's room to get him into trouble. How convenient that one random day, the staff just decided to raid his belongings and discovered the gun and a pack of red pepper. The pepper, they claimed, had been concealed for him to use at a later time in an escape to throw off his scent from any dogs used to chase him. Of course, because of this Byrd was punished severely and kept from being able to write his mother.

Superintendent Hirshberg wrote several letters to Byrd's mother, claiming to be sincere at helping him and also making sure to reiterate that he "was not" keeping Byrd from writing his mother. Eventually the Superintendent grew tired of Byrd's shenanigans and the ward was later deemed *"wholly incorrigible and rebellious, not amendable to discipline and not fit for detention."* Hirshberg then shipped Byrd off to the Court in Santa Clara where he was sent to jail there for the remainder of his sentence.

What I find interesting is that after his ordeal at Preston, Byrd was never incarcerated again. In fact, he later went on to marry and have children and filed several patents with the Government for inventions he made. Byrd went on to work for and own several manufacturing companies including Pajaro Industries and R. E. Byrd Manufacturing in Erie, PA.

Robert had done so well in his business, that in the 1920's his ads were seen published in various editions of Popular Mechanics magazine. During the 1930's and the height of the Depression, Robert's manufacturing business was doing so well that he had over 150 employees working 3 shifts, 7 days per week. Robert's legacy was then passed down to his sons, grandsons and great-grandchildren, who still continue to remain in the manufacturing industry as successful entrepreneurs to this day. Sadly, Robert didn't live a long life, dying at the age of 48 from congestive heart failure and kidney failure.

One good thing that Robert took with him when he left Preston was a trade. Learning how to manufacture the key that he used to escape from Preston, was the catalyst that inspired him later in life to become a manufacturer. Robert E. Byrd's experience at Preston was one of infamy as far as his many escapes, but the real legacy he left behind was the value of hard work and skills he acquired at Preston that catapulted his life into one of great success for the rest of his life.

CHAPTER 6

The Murder of Joseph Morgan

One story that is rarely mentioned, due to having been buried in old news archives, is the death of Joseph Morgan. Morgan was a ward at Preston back in July of 1899. One evening, Joseph Morgan and another friend Louis Siminoff escaped from Preston. Their plan had initially worked, and they had made it as far as Sheldon, located near Elk Grove.

When the staff realized that the pair was missing, Superintendent Hirshberg sent a group of men out to "fetch" the boys. H.H. Budd and Raphael Blair met up with James Carroll, James Kelly and a dog that tracked the escapees down to the farmlands. When the men approached the land where Morgan and Siminoff were hiding, they split up.

James Kelly and Raphael Blair soon found the boys behind a haystack. Siminoff became frightened of getting caught so he remained hidden while Morgan tried to run away. H.H. Budd shouted not to shoot the boy, which testimony from Siminoff confirms, yet both Blair and Kelly shot with their rifle and pistols. One of the bullets from the gun James Kelly had used hit Morgan through the chest and into his lungs.

He was fatally injured, bleeding to death while Kelly handcuffed him a second time. You see when Morgan had initially escaped, he was handcuffed. Although he managed to get one of his hands out of the cuffs during the escape, the other was still attached to his wrist. As he lay there on the ground, coughing up blood until he died, they still had the audacity to cuff him again.

An inquest was held in Elk Grove and witnesses were questioned. The newspaper headlines read *"Unwarranted Killing Of The Reform School Lad-Bitterly Denounced."*

District Attorney Baker filed murder charges against Kelly and also held Major Raphael Blair accountable as well. This would be the first time on record that someone was held accountable for the wrongdoing they did to the wards from Preston. Sadly, the guard was exonerated on all charges and Joseph Morgan's death was long forgotten.

Hirshberg's View On Corporal Punishment

According to the Preston School of Industry's Biennial Report for 1896-1898, the "Corporal Punishment" section reads: *"When low or base things are practiced, it becomes necessary to resort to vigorous punishment, which, however, is inflicted with discretion."*

It goes on to say: *"Punishment is never inflicted without knowledge or authority of the Superintendent, and always in his presence, but never by him."*

Due to the unwanted and unpleasant publicity for the school, Superintendent Hirshberg resigned in December of 1900, leaving the school to the next Superintendent Rev. C.B. Riddick.

Superintendent, Rev. C.B. Riddick

Trades Building Burns Down

In March of 1904, the Trades Building at Preston burned to the ground. It happened around 10 o'clock in the evening, and no one was reported to have died. After all was said and done, the estimated damage to the building was set at $30,000.

From 1900 to 1906 there was only one reported death of a ward at Preston. The young man's name was John Lawne. His cause of death was reported as tuberculosis. He was sent to Fresno County Hospital due to the nature of his illness and reportedly passed away on June 24, 1902. Other than the one death, it seemed that things were finally settling down as far as rumors and reports of mistreatment. According to their Biennial Report, the medical care they were giving wards on the premises was very good for that time period. Of course, these more quiet days would soon end.

In 1903, Superintendent Riddick retired claiming that it was completely voluntary and that any sort of rumors to the contrary were maliciously false. The new Superintendent to be appointed was W.T. Randall. What seemed to be quite strange is that I could not find Randall's name in the biennial report that listed all of the Superintendents up to 1912. It was only through my thorough newspaper archive digging that I found a gap in between the terms of C.B. Riddick and C.H. Dunton and actually located W.T. Randall's information.

It seems that Randall worked at Preston without too much scandal. The only story I could find with his name mentioned was an article stating that an inmate by the name of Joe Pires was wrongfully committed. He filed a petition on the basis of habeas corpus claiming that he was forced to plead guilty to petty larceny to a Justice of the Peace in Santa Barbara. He was never given a trial and the Superior Court just transferred him to Preston. I couldn't find an outcome for this young man's claim.

In November of 1909 W.T. Randall retired, claiming that he wished to devote more time for educational work at Berkeley. Soon after, C.H. Dunton was appointed Superintendent.

CHAPTER 7

Herman Huber's Death & Fake Escape

By 1911, the quiet reputation Preston had started to acquire was then lost again to scandal when a young inmate by the name of Herman Huber was killed in an escape attempt. Herman Huber was born Herman Willis Huber, the grandson of William Ladd Willis, a member of Sacramento high society.

Huber's maternal grandfather had worked in the editorial department of the *Record-Union* in Sacramento for thirteen years and also compiled the 'State Speller' publications for the State Board of Education. Some of his publications for the State Board of Education and Historical publications such as *"History of Sacramento, California"* by W. L. Willis, can still be found in most library archives.

Another tidbit to add to Herman Huber's genealogy shows that his third great-grandfather Lyman Hall was one of the signers of the Declaration of Independence and also a close friend of General Washington.

According to the State Archives in Downtown Sacramento, Herman Huber was received at Preston on December 6, 1910. There is no notation as to what sort of crime or conviction he had, only the word "Delinquent" on the register book. Apparently, he was sentenced to four years at Preston due to the fact his release date was said to be in August of 1914.

On the night of October 17, 1911, around the time when staff was ringing the dinner bell, Herman Huber and another friend, John Kirrane made their escape under the cover of darkness.

According to school officials, the night watchman J.D. French noticed they were gone and went after them. J.D. French also claimed that he shot his gun to warn the Superintendent that an incident was occurring and accidentally shot and killed Huber. Inmate John Kirrane's name was in the newspapers for days following the incident due to the fact he had not been caught. I couldn't find any further records to indicate whether he was ever apprehended or not.

Another inmate, Ernest Reed, who was later paroled that very week, claimed that he witnessed the very shooting and that J.D. French killed Huber deliberately. He came before Governor Hiram Johnson on October 23rd, claiming that Huber was murdered by J.D. French and that C.H. Dunton was also a very cruel and harsh Superintendent on the boys. Reed stated that J.D. French, the shooter, pulled his revolver from his hip and shot him down instantly without pause. He also went on to say:

"The boys who would incur displeasure of the officials at the school, are confined to insanity quarters, flayed on their bare back with a heavy strap and given a bread and water diet, with more water than bread."

If that wasn't bad enough, there was a scandal just a month later involving the Assistant Superintendent and a former woman employee. According to the information I obtained, there was some sort of inappropriate behavior on the part of Asst. William S. Williams of a sexual nature. When brought before the Superintendent, the lady was fired and Asst. Williams was kept employed with no sort of disciplinary action taken. The pastor at Preston was so upset about the wrongdoing that he quickly resigned his position and claimed that he didn't want to be around when an investigation was brought upon the school. Later, Asst. Williams secretly stepped down without telling the State or Board of Trustees. Dunton then hired someone else without authority to do so.

Fake Escapes

I find this case with Herman Huber and Ernest Reed very interesting because at Preston they had a set of guidelines to follow. When a inmate arrived at the school, they were given the chance to earn so many credits a day. After three months if they were not making progress, they would be demoted to a lower company making less credits and receiving less privileges.

Although technically the Biennial Reports state that the credit system didn't officially start until 1912, it appears as if it may have begun as a trial period before they officially implemented it.

If you, as an inmate, were going to school, doing well and maintaining a good attitude, you would be rewarded and promoted to a higher company with more privileges and more credits. In order to leave Preston before the age of 21 (or sometimes 22,) you had to earn 6,500-7,000 credits. If you were critically behind on credits and almost of age to be released then the credit system wouldn't matter to you.

However, if you were 15-17 years old and you wanted to get out early, there was a way of doing it. The boys had figured out the method to do this but it was often 'abused'. You see, "rats" or "stool pigeons" at Preston were greatly rewarded with credits.

If an inmate helped in the capture of another inmate who was escaping they would receive the ultimate reward. This is how it worked. If you told the school that you saw someone escaping or if you aided in actually chasing them down and catching them, you would be paroled automatically because you would earn all your credits in one shot.

Boys who were about to be released, due to their age, sometimes wanted to help out their younger friends by offering to "fake" an escape. They would escape and then have the younger fellow report it to the officer, where then the inmate would be caught. The younger boy would be praised as a hero, given all his credits and paroled early, whereas the "escapee" would be released in the next 6 months or so usually since they couldn't keep him any longer than the maximum age limit.

This is why I believe the death of Herman Huber was a "fake" escape gone terribly wrong. You see, I am convinced that Ernest Reed was the one who told J.D. French about Huber and Kirrane escaping. I think that Reed assumed that the night watchman would go after them, capture them and everything would go as planned.

He didn't think that French would shoot him dead. As for Kirrane, I believe he was so shocked to see his friend shot that he just kept running. That would make sense as to why Reed was a witness to the shooting and why he was paroled just days later.

After Reed testified to the Governor about this scandal, an investigation was brought on Dunton and the School. By February of 1912, another article hit the papers. This time a young ward, by the name of Robert Robertson (age 14), was stabbed multiple times on his sides by Frank Pimentel (age 20) with a pocket knife.

This new incident brought on many more questions as to how a ward managed to obtain a pocket knife and why younger boys were being mixed with older, more hardened criminals. After a lengthy investigation, Dunton resigned from office of Superintendent in June of 1912.

Herman Huber is buried at the Masonic Cemetery (adjoining the old Sacramento City Cemetery) in Sacramento, California.

CHAPTER 8

The Death of Samuel Goins

One story you might have heard while looking into the Preston School of Industry's history, is the story of Sam Goins. Goins was an African-American inmate who was shot by John or J.E. Kelley (also seen spelled as Kelly). Goins was originally from North Carolina, but had been incarcerated in Alameda on a burglary charge prior to his stay at Preston.

According to the *Amador Ledger* dated April, 19, 1919 entitled "Guard Kills P.S.I. Escape" states:

"Samuel Goins, colored, an inmate of the Preston School was fatally shot by guard J.E. Kelley last Saturday. Goins escaped from the school the day before and the guards found him at the Thornton Ranch.

He threatened to kill anyone who attempted to take him. Kelly, failing to halt him by command, fired to hit him in the leg, but just as he pressed the trigger, Goins stooped to go under a wire fence and the bullet struck him in the back.

He lived several hours, and before dying, exonerated the guard, declaring he alone was to blame for the affair.

- 42 -

Kelly was acquitted by the coroner's inquest held Tuesday. The funeral was held in Ione, Wednesday. Goins was a native of North Carolina, aged 20 years. He went to the school from Alameda County for burglary."

Samuel Goins was just two months shy of being released when he attempted his third escape. It was reported in the newspapers that ward J. Lopez, who was with Goins when he died, testified on J.E. Kelly's behalf at the inquest. However, the inquest records state that his name was actually Joe Acosta. Acosta claimed that Goins, "tripped going over the fence and he got shot after he tripped over." Eight months later, a ward by the name of James Lopez died from bronchial pneumonia. He is also buried in the cemetery at Preston.

Who Was J. E. Kelley?

According to census records and Amador County records there were only two men named John Kelly in Ione at the time, and one was named J.E. Kelley or Kelly and the other was J.K. Kelly (who was his son).

I spoke with the grandson of a J.E. Kelly who claimed he had no knowledge of his grandfather being involved in any shooting of an inmate at Preston or that he ever worked there. I also spoke to the Amador County Librarian, Laura, who found the same information as I did about the two men named John Kelly in Amador County.

According to records, one J.E. Kelly was born in 1865 in Plymouth, CA. He was the Constable of Ione for a lengthy period of time according to the old newspaper archives. Another Kelly, J.K. Kelly was only 18 years old at the time of this incident and there is no record of him working for Preston.

When this escape attempt occurred, John E. Kelly would have been about 54 years old. It is quite possible that he had been the Constable and also maintained a presence at Preston for certain incidents such as an escape. This would not be unusual. If you recall, in Chapter 4, when Superintendent O'Brien threatened a young boy from Ione, his guard Officer Phillips was also an Amador County Sheriff Deputy.

So you see, in Amador County at that time, the local authorities and Preston's officers were basically intertwined. Regardless of which Kelly it was, there were only two possibilities in Amador County at the time, so it had to be one or the other.

According to Guard John Kelly's statement, he claims he meant to shoot Goins in the leg and that Goins had waved a hammer towards the other guard Mr. Hunter approaching him prior to his running and ducking under the wire fence. John Kelly went on to say:

"I knew what he told me before, that the next time he ran away whoever tried to catch him would either kill him or he would kill the person that was after him. I seen him watching Mr. Hunter and holding the hammer and I knew he would strike him if he would get a chance. He was nearing a low fence, I should judge it was three feet probably. It was what they call 'hog wire' on the bottom, two barb wires on top.

As he neared the fence, I thought he was going to leap over it because I seen him jump before. He was a good jumper. I raised my gun and was just in the act, when he either tripped or fell as he was about to make the jump, and as I pulled the trigger, that I calculated on him jumping over, he fell through the fence.

We went down to where he was. Mr. Hunter was the first one to him. He went to where he was lying and he said, "Goins, are you hurt?" He said "Yes, sir." I went up to the house to get some water. Mr. Thornton came with me. I asked Mr. Thornton where was the nearest doctor? He first said Burson, but afterward he said Ione was as near.

I wanted to get medical aid for the boy. He said "no." We then laid Mr. Goins in the machine, proceeded to Ione, drove to the doctor's office. The doctor was not in. We then went to the school and left him there at the school and the authorities up there sent for Mr. Gall at Jackson."

After Goins' death, the school made sure his funeral was taken care of and even mentioned it in the local papers. Most of the time when other wards died at Preston, their deaths were basically unmentioned.

Many people speculate that Goins was shot with little to no regard for his life, but I believe that was not the case here. Think about it. He had escaped from Preston and was on the run. He was a fugitive who had escaped in the past and who had already made threats that he would not be taken alive again. He had also threatened that anyone who stood in his way would be taken out as well.

Kelly was aware of Goins' past threats. Upon seeing Goins with a hammer that he had retrieved from a shack on the Thornton ranch, Kelly felt that he had to protect his partner, Mr. Hunter.

Testimony showed that Hunter's opinion was that Goins wasn't really that much of a threat to him at all. Hunter claimed that he was too far from Goins for him to have struck him with the hammer and that Goins was running in front of Hunter. However, from Kelly's perception, Hunter and Goins seemed close in proximity. In the inquest records testimony, Kelly remained adamant that he didn't mean to kill Goins. He claimed that he meant only to wound him in order to stop him.

Several witnesses claimed that they did see Goins trip and fall just as he reached the fence, meaning one of two things. He was either shot and fell on the fence, or Kelly was telling the truth about Goins fall. Perhaps, he did shoot at him while Goins was in the act of attempting to jump the fence but instead tripped and fell, causing the bullet to penetrate his lower back as opposed to the intended target of hitting him in the leg.

Testimony of Dr. A. M. Gall, who examined Goins' body stated that the bullet *"entered the back, mid-way between the lower rib on the left right side and the upper border of the pelvic bone. Passed through, slightly upward and the exit was about two and one-half inches from the sternum and below the last rib."*

Sam Goins later died from his wounds, after claiming that it was no fault of anyone involved, other than his own. He was later buried at the cemetery out behind the "Castle."

His story is one that will always cast doubts in many minds. Did Kelly purposely shoot Goins? Or was it an accident? Did Kelly honestly feel that his partner was in direct danger? Or did he just want to catch Goins whatever means necessary? We may never truly know.

Photo Credit: J'aime Rubio

Photo Credit: Roland Boulware

CHAPTER 9.

Infiltrating The Castle

When I started investigative writing, only one thing was on my mind, revealing the truth. I think I can speak for all reporters and journalists who truly love their jobs, when I say that being a writer is a passion that drives you to do some pretty insane things at times.

One good example, Crime Reporter Scott Thomas Anderson had put himself in harm's way when he spent time traveling the country with various departments of law enforcement to investigate the harsh element of meth driven crime, in his new book "Shadow People."

It's just a known fact that sometimes, in order to get the scoop or just to unravel the pieces of an intricate and enigmatic puzzle of a good mystery, a writer must immerse themselves in the element they are researching. One person that stands out as an original truth seeker, and one who may have very well been the first truth seeker at Preston Castle, was a reporter by the name of Leon Adams.

Photo: S.F. Daily News

In 1923, Adams, a reporter for the San Francisco Daily News, was assigned to investigate the Preston School of Industry undercover as a ward. His assignment was to expose the school for all the terrible things that were being done, not only to the inmates but also within the administration.

In order for Adams to fit in as a real inmate, he had to be arrested and convicted in a criminal court. He was purposely "framed" for attempted burglary, to which he was brought before the court and pled guilty, requesting to be sent to Preston.

In his series of articles exposing the Preston School of Industry's dark secrets of mistreatment and torture, he states:

"Upon seeing Preston at close quarters, one wonders that any boys go "straight" after leaving there. Terrible punishments that impair mentality and physique are administered by officers who are unable to control the youths they guard unless they make an example of every offender."

It was obvious for Adams that the element he had thrust himself into was going to be a tough one to deal with. In his first article, he mentions the fact that he had to get into trouble there, in order to witness firsthand the brutality inflicted on the other wards.

"No one at Preston knew who I was. To reach the cells, I had to "fake." I had my choice of running away, disobeying an officer, assaulting a guard or continued defiance. My pick was the mildest-disobedience.

It wasn't hard. I picked a fight with Jack Hindsman, who always "had a chip on his shoulder." We went to it. I soon found I had picked the wrong opponent, but didn't mind so much. As we fought, the officer stood by and watched.

Fighting is against the rules at Preston, but it didn't matter, there- Capt. J.W. Sibole was enjoying the sight. We finally quit from the exhaustion.

My face was bloody, my lips cut, and both eyes beginning to swell. Looking defiantly at Sibole, I silently dared him to enforce the rule which so often is violated at the school.

He took the dare and ordered the two of us to stand the "guard line." Boys on guard line must stand erect, facing the wall, while others rest. It is a physical punishment. After a few minutes, on the line, I sat down."

As his story went on, he explained that his refusal to stand the line made Sibole angry. Adams was then sent to the detail office to receive a punishment for his insubordination.

When questioned about the fight and his disobedience, Adams refused to answer, thus only getting him into more trouble. He then was sent down the hill to the cell house with his punishment awaiting him, an order to withstand 15 days in solitary confinement.

Photo: P.S.I.

He described the original detention building being too dark and having two tiers of barred doors set in a solid wall made of stone. He states that the doors were fastened in four ways, and each cell having two gates. Windows were high above their reach, also barred. The inner gate was a solid oak lined with quarter-inch steel, while the outer gate was metal.

After being ordered to strip naked and lay face down on the icy cement floor, a guard handed him a piece of canvas that he was supposed to fashion as some sort of undergarment. He then had to follow the guard up the iron ladder to cell No. 22.

"My cell was 10 feet high and 9 feet wide. A faucet, a bowl and an iron bunk, two dirty blankets, a little wad of cloth for a pillow - that was my furniture."

He goes on to mention that the windows had heavy wire screens on them, layers of bars and opaque glass that kept the light out, leaving the inmates in total darkness, day or night.

"My tomb, I called the place. It was the tomb of many boys before me. Scratches on the wall revealed the presence there of an assemblage of notables, names were followed by crosses. Some even counted up to 13 and 14- evidently the number of days a prisoner had spent in the place.

I didn't spend the full 15 days in the cell. Watson took me out on the 11th day, when I was too sick to sit up and reach for the cup of skimmed milk that came through the little hole in the thick cell door.

> *For the first three days I only received one thin slice of bread, one cup half full of thin milk, shoved at me by a hand belonging to a face I never saw. On the fourth day, came a dish of cold meat, cold gravy and cold potatoes. That night I became deathly sick. I think I cried out once, but don't remember much about that. The nights that followed weren't quite so bad. I hadn't enough strength to cry out much more."*

Adams' account of his eleven days in solitary ended with the guard removing him from the cell and forcing him to "stand the line" for ten hours. The first night they forced him to do such a thing, he fainted. For that, they made him stand even longer the next day.

In his article Adams' makes a moving statement: *"What earthly good can come to a boy in a cell? What human ever was worth a straw whose spirit was broken?"*

That statement rings true in so many ways. It was apparent to him that the disciplinary actions or rehabilitation that Preston was inflicting on their wards was doing more harm than good.

In Adams' article *"Youths Kept in Dark Basement,"* he goes on to state that the Administration building's basement was being used to hold 50 boys in the dark. He also mentions that the basement held six solitary confinement cells where boys had been kept for weeks at a time while there was also a flogging room to beat the boys.

It seemed that although Preston was content with their methods of punishing the boys, that the results weren't really making a positive effect on anyone at all.

The statistics alone were proving that Adams' opinions were correct. The boys who endured any time at Preston were leaving the place more corrupted than when they had arrived in the first place.

In his exposé of Preston's goings on, he revealed the following statistics from that time period:

"Only two out of every 100 boys who were taught trades at Preston School of Industry follow those trades after being released.

Ninety boys over every hundred who leave Preston are back again in some state institution within five years.

Seven of the 127 prisoners in the San Francisco jail today, were at Preston at some time or another Out of every 100 criminals at San Quentin State Prison, four are "graduates" of Preston.

Many of California's most notorious crooks received their "education" at the reform school."

In his published articles, Adams revealed not only the harsh treatment but also the filthy living conditions, proof of the managerial incompetence of the Superintendent and also his advice on the measures that should be taken to make the necessary changes for improving the school.

When Superior Court Judge Louis H. Ward had heard of Adams' experience at Preston he felt so moved with emotion that he was quoted saying:

"I'll never feel comfortable again in my conviction that I am doing right when I commit a boy to a reform school."

Thankfully, a man in his position of authority had been reached and moved by the proof Adams had been able to expose about Preston. Unfortunately, the school seemed to be untouchable, even after all that exposure and not much changed over the years. With all that Adams went through in order to shed light and truth for the world to see, unfortunately, as many stories related to Preston, this one was long forgotten in the archives, waiting for someone like me to find it.

Although there may have been many writers, like myself, who have written about Preston Castle and its mysteries, Adams was the one who paved the way. He was the first truth-seeker to expose Preston and call them on all the horrendous things they were doing to those boys. For that, I tip my hat to Leon Adams and his incredible journalism.

CHAPTER 10

The Cemetery - The Boys Buried at Preston

Upon investigating the wards buried in the cemetery behind Preston Castle, I was only able to find a few stories or bits of information in regards to them. Below are the names, dates of birth and death, along with causes of death and any other information I was able to dig up on the boys.

Adolf Antron
1/22/1877-2/20/1895
Cause of Death: Pulmonary Edema
Adolph Antron was the son of working class parents, P.Antron and O. Antron of England and brother to George, Joe, Annie and Ed. The 1880 Census shows that Adolph and his family were living in San Francisco at the time. Adolph's father and mother immigrated from England, however they made stops in France, the Philippine Islands and later onto California where they had children in each country as their place of birth states on the Census. Adolph and his younger brother Ed were the only ones in the family born in the United States.

Grant Walker
7/15/1886 - 6/17/1895
Cause of Death: Typhoid Fever

William C. Williams
8/26/1879 - 6/6/1897
Cause of Death: Acute Meningitis
William C. Williams came from Red River, Van Buren, Arkansas. The 1880 Census shows him as being one year old. His parents were W.H. Williams and Mary Williams. He was the youngest brother to Martha, James and John.

Nicholas Hamilton
1/13/1878 - 5/17/1898
Cause of Death: Pulmonary Tuberculosis
Nicholas Hamilton was Ward/Inmate # 0170. He was first sent to Preston in 1895. In November of 1897, Nicholas Hamilton was thrust into the spotlight after Bernard and Amador County Physician E. E. Endicott filed an affidavit sent to the Governor explaining his witnessing Superintendent O'Brien abusing and torturing the boy after a failed escape attempt that injured his ankle. Only about six months later Hamilton died under suspicious circumstances. The school claimed he had tuberculosis and had been confined in "solitary" quarters, later dying of his illness, however there is really no way to know for sure. Had he really been that ill with such a contagious disease, the school would have known about it earlier and would have sent him to the State Hospital which was protocol. I truly doubt the Superintendent would have even touched him with a ten foot pole, had he known he was ill. No, I do not believe he died of natural causes.

Frank Ward
Unknown -7/17/1898
Cause of Death: Paralytic Dementia

Woolrich Leonard Wooldridge
5/23/1880 - 10/17/1899
Cause of Death: Acute Cerebral Meningitis

Hugh Simms
6/4/1893 - 2/5/1912
Cause of Death: Tuberculosis
Hugh Simms' death was from natural causes. The 1910 Census states that he was a prisoner at the Kern County Jail in Bakersfield before being sent to Preston. His employment history stated he had previously been employed as a cook in Bakersfield.

Roy Scoville
9/14/1895 - 4/29/1913
Cause of Death: Meningitis

Eddie Heath
7/19/1894 - 5/13/1913
Cause of Death: Myocarditis

John Miller
8/13/1898 - 6/13/1913
Cause of Death: Meningitis

Joseph Howe
10/20/1897—12/11/1913
Cause of Death: Tuberculosis

Peter Miller
6/28/1897 - 1/20/1914
Cause of Death: Stroke of Apoplexy

Tehama Vann
7/3/1898 - 6/6/1914
Cause of Death: Accidental Drowning
According to reports discovered by Tim Ferry, Tehama accidentally drowned in the old swimming pond. On June 6, 1914, the boys from Company I and their accompanying Captain J.H. Enright, went down to the pond to swim about twenty minutes after finishing supper. Captain Enright had told all the boys that if they weren't good swimmers to stay at the shallow end of the pond. Tehama had told the boys he could swim, "dog fashion," just before he dove headfirst off the diving board.

They said he came up once for air and raised his hands and arms up in a panic. They tried to grab hold of him, however they didn't reach him in time. He sank to the bottom of the pond. Robert Rains dove in after him several times, along with Albert Rubidoux. However, they could not reach him. The next morning they went out to the pond with poles and a raft, trying to reach his body that way. They eventually found his body and retrieved him, later burying him in the cemetery. The coroner's report and interviews with witnesses confirmed that he had drowned accidentally.

Benjamin Kealohi
5/13/1897 - 6/17/1915
Cause of Death: Acute Nephritis, Peritonitis, Appendicitis rupture.

Samuel Goins
6/24/1899 - 4/19/1919
Cause of Death: Shot while escaping
As stated in my previous chapter, Samuel Goins was shot during his third and final escape attempt. He was just two months shy of his release date when he died.

James Lopez (J. Lopez)
4/7/1903 - 12/23/1919
Cause of Death: Bronchial Pneumonia
Originally brought to court for "dependency" in 1914, only because his mother was unfit to care for him, James jumped from one boys home to the next, until ending up at the Whittier School of Boys and then later transferred to Preston on July 24, 1918.

It was alleged that he was one of the wards who testified on behalf of the guard who shot Samuel Goins during an escape attempt, although the name of the witness on official records was Joe Acosta, not James Lopez.

Frank Aljers (Frank Alves)
3/1/1905 - 5/13/1922
Cause of Death: Abscess of Brain; motorcycle accident
Historian John Lafferty was kind enough to email me his finding on Frank's death. Frank was originally injured in his hometown of Fruitville, California on March 28, 1922. He arrived at Preston on May 6, 1922, where he was immediately sent to the school's hospital. He died a week later. It is unknown why he was ordered to Preston while in such a poor state physically.

Raydell Holliday
1/31/1909-3/23/1929
Cause of Death: Influenza, Rheumatic Fever, Heart Disease

Over the many years that the Preston School was open, there were several deaths of the wards, many of which were not buried on the property but instead their bodies were returned home to their families to be buried elsewhere. It's hard to fathom all the death that place has truly seen.

CHAPTER 11.

Who Really Killed Anna Corbin?

You can look near and far, and search the internet until your heart is content and you will not find as much research about this lady as I have dug up. There have been many sites that speak of Anna Corbin yet no one has revealed anything about her life prior to her death. You see, when I learned about the untimely death of Mrs. Anna Corbin at Preston Castle, I noticed that no one could really say who she was or what her life was like. It was almost as if the ghost stories took on a life of their own.

BRUTALLY SLAIN—Mrs. Anna Corbin, 52, of Ione (above) head housekeeper at the Preston School of Industry, was murdered yesterday in her office at the school.

For some apparent reason people seemed to be far more interested in what happened after Anna's death, rather than what happened before her death. I was determined to find out the story behind Anna Corbin's life no matter what, and that is exactly what I did.

Anna's Earlier Years

Anna Corbin was born on January 16, 1898 in Kansas as Anna Laura Lawton. She was the daughter of Etta Edna Little (1865-1945) and Wilber Austin Lawton (1857-1936) of Americus, Kansas. Her parents were farmers, although Wilber had also been a banker, postmaster, politician, Justice of the Peace, Under-Sherriff and member of the School Board during his lifetime.

As a child, Anna went with her older sister, Loverna, to live with their aunt and uncle in order to attend school in Emporia, Kansas. In fact, they lived just across the street from the famous author/editor William Allen White. Loverna would babysit White's children when he and his wife would travel. White was such a profound influence on Anna's sister that she became a writer herself and published several children's books in her lifetime. It was said that White introduced Loverna, and possibly Anna, to President Theodore Roosevelt.

After graduating from Emporia High School, Anna met and married Robert Travis Corbin in 1918. A year later a son, Harold Jay Corbin was born in 1919. Since Robert T. Corbin was a truck driver it seemed to have made them move around quite a bit. They moved to Colorado where their daughter Avis M. Corbin was born in 1924.

The US Census Records for 1930 shows that by that

time they had moved to Whittier, California (East Los Angeles). The records show Robert as being 34 years old, Anna being 32, Harold 11, and Avis 6. Sometime around 1935 they relocated to Ione, California. Shortly thereafter, Robert was hired at Preston as a group Supervisor while Anna was later hired as a housekeeper.

In 1941, both Robert T. Corbin and his son Harold Jay Corbin were listed on draft registers during WWII. In 1943, Harold Jay Corbin, only 24 years old, was killed in action during the war when his plane was shot down over France.

Harold's name is featured as one of the first Amador County residents who were killed in action while serving in the military on the recently made War Veterans Memorial in Ione. He was stationed out of Presidio of Monterey, Army Air Force (2LT # 0-666635). He was buried March 14, 1950 at Golden Gate National Cemetery in San Bruno, California.

Social Security Death Index records indicate Robert died on May 29, 1947 in Napa, California. He is buried at East Lawn Cemetery in Sacramento.

Let's try to step into Anna's shoes for a moment, shall we? Now imagine you are a middle aged woman, a wife and mother. Imagine that both your son and husband had recently died. Anna's parents had died as well years prior. Now how would you feel inside? Think about it.

There she was, the only parent left for her newly married daughter Avis. How do you think she felt? Now imagine, it is 1950, and here she was not only grieving for two of the most important men in her life but she also had to work full time as a head housekeeper as her only means of support.

Think about this also. Her son Harold died in 1943 and yet the US Air Force had not brought his body back to be buried until 1950. His internment was March 14, 1950, a whole month after Anna's death. So in her lifetime she was never able to visit her son's grave or know exactly what happened to his body in order to find closure. That must have been agonizing to say the least. I am a mother and I know for a fact losing a child, at any age would be devastating.

Harold Corbin (third from left) and his crew
Photo: Loren Bender

To make things even more sad, on the very day of Anna's murder, a telegram from the War Department was sent out to Anna, notifying her that her son Harold's body was being returned to the U.S. for burial. The telegram arrived too late. She didn't live long enough to ever learn what happened to her son's body.

So here it was 1950, and Anna was by then the head housekeeper at Preston School of Industry. She had been working there for 15 years according to the Superintendent's statement. Anna's husband's draft enlistments state that he was working at Preston at the time the enlistment card was written and that date was 1941. More than likely her and her husband were both hired at the same time in 1935.

Another tidbit to add, Anna did not live in an apartment in the building she was murdered in. She lived in five-bedroom house in Ione. She did not live in the Administration building as so many reports and television shows claim. The papers claimed she lived on Marquette St (which doesn't exist), so either she lived on Market St. or Marlette Street in Ione. Either way, Anna did not live at Preston.

The Day of the Murder

It was Thursday, February 23, 1950. Just before a staff meeting held by the Superintendent Robert B. Chandler, a ward, Robert Hall, along with housekeeper Lillian Lee McDowall, discovered the body on Anna Corbin and quickly notified the staff of the grisly finding.

Prior to entering Anna Corbin's office, they noticed the door leading outside of the building was open. Hall claimed that he discovered blood stains on the door jam leading out of Anna's office and a blood trail that led them to the supply room. Hall claimed, "*Something stopped the door from opening full swing. It was a large clothes hamper. I moved it and there was a large pool of blood on the floor underneath. There was a lot of blood on the door leading to the storage room. It was locked with a padlock."*

According to Hall's account, he kicked the door in and went into the room. The ward noticed that in the large 16 ft. long by 35 ft. wide room, that contained a pile of carpeting in the corner that was out of place. Hall quickly went over to the carpet and pulled them aside to discover the ghastly sight of poor Mrs. Corbin's body dead, in a half-sitting position. The blood trails from the different rooms convinced investigators that it was possible that there were two killers. They believed she had been first attacked in her office, and then dragged through the supply room into the adjoining storeroom. Someone had used an undershirt to attempt to wipe up the pools of blood on the floor, smearing it. The shirt was an old one, so it was more than likely used as a dust rag in cleaning.

Anna's clothes were mangled leading the authorities to assume she had either been raped prior or even possibly after being murdered. Another bit of information leaked to the press was that Anna's body was found with shoe polish on her undergarments. The autopsy report later revealed that she had not been sexually assaulted.

The Suspects

The last person who claimed to have seen Anna alive was the Head Gardener, Jeff Machado. He stated that he had brought Anna acacia branches and blossoms around 9-9:30 a.m. Another housekeeper, Elizabeth Goodman stated that around 10:23 a.m. she came into Anna's office and left an apple on her desk. That apple was still there upon the discovery of Anna's body.

Lillian McDowall and her helper/ward Robert Hall were the ones to discover Anna's body a little after 1:30 p.m. The Coroner stated that she had been dead for at least four hours when her body was discovered, leading many to believe that she died between 9 a.m. and 10 a.m. that morning.

Initially the Superintendent, along with Sheriff Lucot and other investigators singled out the 22 wards on "housekeeping detail" before questioning other wards who had been convicted of assault and sexual crimes. After those groups were questioned, they detained all wards to their rooms for further questioning and investigation of each one.

Superintendent Chandler made it very clear that everyone was a suspect at that point. He even stated that the staff would be investigated thoroughly. Ultimately, there were three wards who were found to be actual "suspects".

A handwritten letter addressed to Superintendent Chandler stated that Anna's killer was not a ward, but in fact a member of the staff who "wanted her job, but didn't make the cut." The name of the sender was Mrs. Melissa Benn of West Sacramento. Although Mrs. Benn made these claims that she knew who Anna's murderer was, she offered no further information nor did she give the name of the person.

Another question that arose was in regards to Anna's keys being left on her desk. The Superintendent went on to say that it was a "Cardinal Offense" to leave your keys lying around and that Anna would never, in all the years she had worked there, have left her keys out on the desk that way intentionally.

There were no clues that any blood had been left on the keys. This implied that that the killer did not use Anna's keys to lock her in the store room that was adjacent to the supply room and then return the keys back to her desk. Of course, there is really is no way to know.

The idea about the keys would make someone wonder about a staff member possibly being involved in her death. In my search, I could not find anything that said whether or not the wards on housekeeping detail may have been able to use keys under the supervision of a housekeeper.

Avis Barone, Anna's daughter, claimed that she had letters from her mother and also excerpts found in Anna's diary that pointed to a few boys on her housekeeping detail that she felt were possible suspects in her mother's death. One boy in particular was none other than Robert Hall, the very boy who discovered her body.

According to Avis, on August 16, 1949, Anna had written her a letter stating :

"We took a sharp-bladed knife from each of the two of our house squad boys. Just now one of the same boys asked me what I would do if a boy threatened me with a knife. I just said, 'I don't scare easy, Upton.' He said, 'Against a knife you wouldn't have a chance.' However I didn't act scared, I guess, for he started talking about other things then..."

The very same day that Anna had written her daughter that letter, she had also written this entry in her diary: "August 16, 1949—I'm rather concerned about the threatening letter from my boy, Robert Hall."

Avis told the newspapers, "Mother told me two boys had tried to make love to her, and that Upton wanted to marry her. Mother told him she was old enough to be his mother."

It was obvious that both ward Upton and ward Robert Hall were a bit obsessed with Anna to the point that she was sincerely concerned about her safety. Anna was described by many as a beautiful lady. She had even modeled in a fashion show for the Community Methodist Church in Ione the night before she was killed. Her petite 5'2 frame, her dark hair, very neatly dressed appearance and the fact she looked at least 10 years younger than she was probably only added to the unwanted attention the wards gave her. The day of her death she was dressed in a brown dress with a beige sweater that buttoned up the front, she was not in some sort of housekeeper uniform as many may assume.

While Hall remained a person of interest in the case, the authorities failed to charge him despite the information Anna's daughter provided. Avis and her aunt, Loverna Morris, made it known to the press how thoroughly disgusted they were with the school and how they ran things.

Loverna stated, *"I am not interested in revenge. Punishment of the guilty is not my concern, either. But I think those in authority have a responsibility of providing more adequate facilities and personnel so this thing cannot happen again."*

Avis went on to say, *"If nothing comes out of this investigation, if the administration doesn't do something to make it better or safer for those who work there, then her death will have been in vain."*

Upon the discovery of Anna's body, the authorities started a 104-hour probe of suspects and evidence that failed to yield any progress in the case. Sheriff Lucot and the State Investigators that were called out to work the case constantly butted heads throughout the entire ordeal. Eventually, out of the entire staff and the 657 wards questioned, in the end only one person was charged as a suspect. That person's name was Eugene Monroe.

Newspaper clipping of Eugene Monroe

Eugene Monroe

Monroe was a 19 year old African-American inmate who was from Southern California. What some people did not know was that he had been a suspect in a murder of a 17 year old female in Los Angeles just a few years prior to Anna's murder. At the time, he was using the alias Eugene Jefferson, his step-father's last name.

In 1947, the body of Vesta Belle Sapenter was found dead in her upstairs bedroom at her home. Detective Raleigh R. Coppage of the LAPD, reported that the girl's lifeless body was found with a piece of rope tightened about her neck, tied in a square knot. She had also been raped.

According to Vesta Sapenter's brother's statement to the police, he claimed that he had come home to find Monroe delivering furniture to their home. Monroe then asked Carlisle if he could use the restroom. After he agreed, Monroe headed upstairs and then later came back down. Carlisle asked Monroe if he had seen his sister, which Monroe replied, "she's upstairs." He also later replied he hadn't seen her at all.

Monroe and Carlisle then headed upstairs and to Vesta's bedroom door, which happened to be locked. Carlisle broke the door down and discovered his sister's body. Apparently she had been hanging curtains on the windows when she was attacked.

What is interesting to note is that the knot used to strangle Vesta was the same type of knot used in Anna's murder. In the Corbin case, the knot had been pulled up tight behind the left ear, which was the exact place they found the knot on Vesta. Although they interrogated Monroe, the police had no proof to hold him.

"I am certain this boy did the job, but we were just never able to prove it. He was the only one in the house at the time and had ample time to commit the act," Coppage stated for the press. Although he was a suspect in that murder, he was released and later ended up at Preston for a conviction of burglary charges.

Upon Monroe's arrival, the Preston School was quite well aware of Monroe's mental issues and violent behavior. In fact, it was even admitted that Monroe should have never been sent to Preston in the first place. Superintendent

Chandler was well aware of the risk he was taking by allowing Monroe at Preston, let alone allowing him to be on "cleaning detail," which was something that was swept under the rug after Anna's death made headlines.

In fact, Monroe was assigned to cleaning detail that was within 200 feet of Anna on the day of her murder. Most people aren't aware of this because it was covered up for years. Monroe should have been locked away in the Tamarack Lodge building which held the solitary confined inmates. He was constantly destroying the cells he was placed in. Some of the acts he had committed included ripping mattresses apart, tearing pipes off the walls and literally destroying anything and everything including his skin. Yes, he even used self mutilation as a form of violent behavior.

I spoke to a few old timers about this case. One who had worked at Preston and another who knew Anna and her family. They had been around during the time of the trial. One also knew classified information regarding the case. Even after all this time, these men still don't want their names revealed because of the fact that they believe the State of California had been involved in helping with the cover up. I have honored their wishes and kept their names anonymous.

When Anna's body was found, Chandler knew the repercussions that would come down on Preston swiftly and harshly. This was due to the fact he allowed such a violent and dangerous ward to work in the administration building with little to no supervision. He had to quickly cover it up.

William J. Mercer, a fellow ward and a self-claimed witness stated that he knew Monroe murdered Anna. Mercer claimed that he saw Monroe argue with Anna, whereas he then struck her face twice with his fists. In a panic, Mercer fled the scene and returned to the hospital where he claimed he felt ill. Upon Mercer's request, he was moved to the Amador County jail out of fear for his life. A civil rights attorney involved with the NAACP, licensed in Sacramento was then called in to represent Monroe. You see, if the school could keep Monroe from being convicted, then obviously it would leave a question in everyone's mind that someone other than Monroe could have committed the crime. If they could cast that shadow of a doubt, the liability of having such a dangerous ward like Monroe wouldn't fall on their shoulders as harshly.

The prosecution's witness, Mercer, had insinuated that Eugene had wanted to have a secretive homosexual relationship with him, and that during a time when they were about to engage in a sex act that Anna had walked in and witnessed them. He claimed that it infuriated Eugene and he said he was going to kill her for that.

After a short visit from Monroe's attorney at the Amador County Jail, Mercer recanted the statement. Later, during the actual trial, Mercer claimed that the statement he originally gave authorities about the murder was true, but that Monroe's defense attorney had threatened that if Mercer didn't change his story, that Eugene Monroe's friends would kill him when he was released. Because of his going back and forth with his statements, Mercer's testimony didn't seem to be taken as "credible," despite the fact he was probably telling the truth.

It was stated that the wards were shocked and infuriated that Anna had been killed. The wards themselves were even reported to have told the staff that if the assailant was found within Preston, that they better hire more guards because the inmates may "*take the law into their own hands*" in order to avenge the death of their beloved housekeeper and motherly friend, Anna Corbin.

Mercer had also implied that he witnessed Eugene burning his clothes in the incinerator. Other comments had been made that Monroe was seen trying to polish his shoes over and over to get the blood off of them. Also, a belt that allegedly belonged to Eugene had been found with blood on it as well. Since Anna and Monroe had the same blood type, they could not conclusively tie the blood on his shoes or belt to the crime scene.

Monroe faced two trials in Amador County, both ending in a hung jury. In the second trial, the jury voted 11-1 for conviction. The one juror who caused the mistrial, Lynwood Miner, claimed he needed police protection due to the fact that people were throwing rocks in the windows of his home after the trial was over. The D.A. was still adamant about holding a re-trial but defense attorney Colley, requested that the third trial be moved out of the county and instead take place in Sacramento. The outcome of the final trial ended in a full acquittal of Monroe. He was now a free man.

During the preliminary part of my investigation of Eugene Monroe, I didn't think he had killed Anna Corbin. Originally, I had my suspicions that it must have been a staff member or even quite possibly a guard. This had been because there had been so many stories of the brutality that the guards inflicted upon the wards at Preston. It wasn't until I discovered so many more facts surround-

-ing Vesta Sapenter's murder, along with information of another murder committed after Anna's death, that I was fully convinced of Eugene Monroe's guilt. I now believe that he did in fact kill Anna Corbin.

After Eugene was free, he traveled to Tulsa, OK. in 1951. After being picked up on a lesser crime, Monroe was caught boasting and bragging in an intercepted note to another inmate that he was the "hottest thing in town," criminally speaking of course. At the time there had been a highly publicized murder of a young pregnant woman by the name of Dorothy Waldrop.

Waldrop was a young wife and former dance teacher of the Murray Dance Studio in St. Joseph, OK. She was home the day of her murder while her husband, Robert, was working as a taxi driver in Tulsa.

Monroe's fingerprints were later found on the venetian blinds that had been ripped off the window in Dorothy's apartment. They were found a short distance from her body on a grassy hillside near her home. She had been raped and choked to death.

An FBI check was done on Monroe while he was in jail under different charges. This was after he bragged to a cellmate that he was a "sought after criminal" in one of the biggest unsolved murder case in the area at that time. Two younger boys who were outside near Dorothy's home at the time of her murder came forward and claimed they had seen a man driving near where Dorothy's body was later found. They stated that the man was in a car with California plates and they also heard a woman screaming.

When looking further into this, the press implied that the Oklahoma Police had beaten a confession out of him. They stated that his eyes had been tortured and he had bruises and scratches on his face. One would assume that he had been coerced into giving a confession, just as Defense Attorney Colley claimed that the authorities had attempted to do in the Corbin case. Witness accounts in Amador County tell a different story, claiming that it was Monroe who was completely unstable during his interrogation prior to being sent to the Amador County Jail. If you recall, Monroe was one who became very violent and erratic, often hurting himself at times. This would explain why he came out of interrogation in Tulsa with scratches on his face and a tortured look. More than likely, this was self inflicted.

After learning the facts surrounding Anna Corbin's murder, Vesta Sapenter's murder and Dorothy Waldrop's murder, this led me to conclude there could only be one person responsible, Eugene Monroe. In 1951, Eugene was convicted and confessed to the murder and rape of Dorothy Waldrop. No one is sure why Eugene decided to kill her but he did admit that he forced her out of her apartment and killed her. Monroe claimed a friend named Eugene McDaniel also aided in the crime.

Although Monroe stood to face the death penalty, he was only sentenced to life imprisonment. Oklahoma Department of Corrections, Inmate Number # 53479, Eugene Monroe only spent 29 years in prison. He was received at the State Prison in 1952 and was later paroled on April 25, 1981.

According to Kevin Moore with the Department of Corrections in Oklahoma, Monroe went on to California and remained on "inactive parole" for many years. Eventually he was considered "missing" between 2002-2009. The officer who was assigned to track Monroe realized his date of birth being January 31, 1931 and recognized he was quite elderly in age. He then decided to do a check in the Social Security death index and found that Eugene Monroe died in Los Angeles in October of 2007.

Final Goodbye To Anna

The day before Anna was killed she appeared in the "Community Fashion Show" in Ione, as one of the models on the cat walk. She was a cheerful and happy person who tried to make the best of her situation. It was obvious by the way the community, the staff at Preston and the inmates spoke of her, that she was well liked within inside and outside of Preston. This terrible tragedy was not only a horrific story but also a sad tale for all who knew her and loved her, including many of the inmates. To this day, I have spoken to several people who once served time at Preston and nearly everyone states how sad they were to know that an innocent woman, such as Anna, died on those premises. Even after her death, her motherly reputation lived on through word of mouth over the generations of inmates coming in and out of that place.

Anna Corbin
Photo: Oakland Tribune

I originally wrote my blog about Anna Corbin several years ago. My opinions were based on the information I had at the time. I had my assumptions in the beginning that it might have been a staff member who had murdered her, or even possibly an unknown suspect that had not even been mentioned before. During my research I was given some leads by a few older citizens of Amador County. They stated that there was such an person who should have never stepped foot on those grounds. The school was well aware of the danger he posed on anyone in his path and yet they turned a blind eye to that danger. The inmate was, in fact, Eugene Monroe.

After several years of thoroughly researching the life of Eugene Monroe, and meticulously going over the facts surrounding all three murder cases, I am convinced Monroe was guilty of all three crimes; However, technically the Corbin case is still considered "unsolved."

Anna Corbin's grave can be found at East Lawn Cemetery in Sacramento.

J'aime Rubio at
Anna Corbin's grave

CHAPTER 12.

A Senseless Death of the Agricultural Teacher

Another story that has been whispered around the County for years is that of the death of 45 year old Vocational Agriculture Instructor, James Wieden after a brutal attack that took place on December 2, 1965.

Wieden just happened to be at the wrong place at the wrong time it seems. It turns out that the two inmates, William Dunlap and Robert Stalcup, planned on making an escape by volunteering to stay after their regular vocational class and help Wieden weld a trailer hitch. They planned on taking advantage of being the only ones out there at the time besides Wieden.

Dunlap admitted to bludgeoning Wieden over the head with a metal pipe the size of a baseball bat, near the machine shop. Apparently, before attempting to flee, they decided that Wieden was in their way, so they chose to kill him. Both inmates were eventually caught and later pled guilty to charges of second degree murder.

After speaking to a few old timers in Amador County, I was told that James Wieden didn't actually die on the grounds of Preston. He was badly hurt, and taken to the hospital where he later died of his injuries on December 5th.

James Wieden is buried at Cherokee Memorial Park in Lodi, California. Later on, the California Youth Authority Facility at Preston, named their high school after James Wieden in honor of the fallen teacher.

CHAPTER 13.

Famous and Infamous Inmates

Among the many inmates who have come and gone from the Preston School of Industry, some have left their mark in history becoming famous or infamous.

Some of the more famous people remembered for their time at Preston consist of country singer and songwriter Merle Haggard, radio and TV personality Eddie Anderson, actor Rory Calhoun, boxers Don Jordan and Eddie Machen, tennis star Pancho Gonzalez, actor Eddie Bunker, bantamweight contender Keeny Teran, screenwriter Ernest Booth, "Seventh Step Rehab" writer Bill Sands, prison minister Phil Thatcher and award winning author Art Rodriguez.

Art Rodriguez at Preston

Some of the more infamous inmates include serial killer Gerald Armond Gallego, death row celebrity author Caryl Chessman, Ray Johnson and the bank robber who is most notably remembered for his role in "The Battle at Alcatraz," inmate Joseph Paul Cretzer. Also included was gangster Allen Smiley, and Prohibition rum runner and builder of The Stardust Resort & Casino in Las Vegas, Tony Cornero.

Art Rodriguez

In his book "East Side Dreams," author Art Rodriguez spoke freely of his time spent at Preston. He spoke of how the inmates were separated based on aptitude tests, basically classifying the inmates into different categories: manipulators, leaders or followers.

"One day about two weeks after arriving at Preston, they told me I was classified as a CFM [Follower]. Some guys were leaders, others manipulators. These prisoners were always trying to con us out of something! They grouped all the guys of one classification together in the same company. One can imagine how it would be if the officials were right in their classifications. If leaders were all put together and thought of bad things to do, how could they lead the followers who were placed together in a separate company? I was a CFM. I don't remember what that stands for, but it means follower. If somebody would say "let's go rob a bank," I was supposed to say, "OK, let's go!" With all the aptitude tests I had to take, I never thought they had it right."

Art goes on in his book to mention the gangs, violence and dangers that were part of being at Preston. He spoke of the lack of qualified or competent educators in the school, even admitting taking advantage of his teacher in one instance. Mr. Williams, who should have been long since retired due to his age, loss of hearing and unfortunate incompetency, was fooled by Art to change the credits on Art's education files.

Basically, Art pulled a fast one over on the teacher in order to receive enough credits to graduate. By pretending that he had shorted credits from previous semesters, despite the fact that Art hadn't even been in Preston that long, he had convinced the teacher that he had made an error thus talking him into "fixing" his papers. Art's experience at Preston wasn't always so easy, being that many times after being involved in fights, he was thrown in "lock up" and even hospitalized after a foolish glue sniffing incident that left one of his friends dead.

During his stay at Preston, he faced many new experiences, including learning to write and spell. He also learned that Preston, with all its harsh elements, was no place for him. I believe his time spent there taught him that he didn't want to continue the course he was on. Upon his release of Preston, he recalled the memory of leaving on the bus as it drove down the road leading out of Ione. There were stories told between the inmates that if you looked back at Preston as you left, it meant you were doomed to return again. Art chose not to look back, and he never did return there.

He went on to be a successful business owner, caring husband and father, but more importantly he became an award winning author who touched the lives of many youths who grew up in the same "institutionalized" lifestyle.

By Art's example, he was able to influence many young lives for the better, by encouraging them to stay away from the gang life and focus on more positive possibilities. His book, "East Side Dreams," has become a staple in many schools, teaching kids that actions always come with consequences. In the hopes of deterring them from making the same mistakes, Art put his whole heart into continuing his lifelong effort by helping others.

"East Side Dreams," was honored as one of the "Best Teenage Books" in the United States by the New York Public Library System, also winning First Place in the Latino Literary Hall of Fame for "Best Cover Illustration & Best First Book."

Art Rodriguez passed away on April 4, 2010.

In 2011, he was posthumously awarded for "Best Young Adult Nonfiction" at the International Latino Book Awards (2011). Art Rodriguez is a prime example, just like former Preston ward Robert E. Byrd, that despite the harsh circumstances of life, one still has the choice to come out of it a better person.

Art Rodriguez

CHAPTER 14

Final Thoughts

I have learned so very much during the time that I have spent researching Preston's history. I know for a fact there are dozens of stories I haven't covered. As it seems, my job devoted to uncovering the history of Preston will never be complete. From what I have found, I have discovered the transformation of a certain former inmate to a caring and compassionate man, whose dream was to help and positively influence young boys towards a better life. I have also seen how power and authority, when given to the wrong person, can be devastating and fatal in many cases.

Man has the natural inclination to want to rule over people with an iron fist. Some men are better than others with controlling that thirst for power, while others cannot.

The crimes of cruelty and harsh mistreatment were massive. To see it continued over the course of many decades shows me that Preston was a dark and painful place in which to be committed. There were reports from wards incarcerated there that rape, sodomy, torture, starvation and mental abuse were rampant and constant occurrences over the entire time that Preston was a functioning facility. The harsh treatment and mental abuse even led a few boys into committing suicide.

I feel so badly for the boys who came there. Some of which who weren't even criminals, left jaded and forever tarnished because of the negative element they were forced to endure.

I know that not all the boys at Preston were perfect little angels because many were there for serious offenses. However, I do feel that if this place would have been more positive and nurturing like the way it had been set out to be, that the boys there would have flourished rather than wilt like dead blossoms.

There was so much prejudice and ignorance on the part of the officials working there at the time that I am sure the boys left that place with scars of low self-esteem as well as physical ones. The majority of the boys were labeled as morons, imbeciles and retarded. As I read the notes from their Biennial Reports, I just shook my head at the complete nonsense as to how they concluded such things.

Many of these boys learned how to manipulate the credit system there by their "fake escapes." That doesn't sound like a moron to me. What about Robert E. Byrd, the one who manufactured a key in order to escape? A person of less intelligence could not do something so clever. Byrd went on to live a good life, never again going to jail and later owning several manufacturing companies and patenting many inventions.

It is sad to think how brainwashed some of these boys may have become after being told or treated as though they were less intelligent than others. It saddens me even more to think of what the original Superintendent of Preston Castle, E. Carl Bank, would have to say had he seen all that took place at this school for so many years.

From the start of Preston, it became tarnished with the reputation for brutality and cruelty which continued to maintain that infamous reputation up until the very end. Even after the "Castle" had been long closed, the newer facility became known for their harsh treatment and brutality until the state finally shut them down.

For over 115 years Preston could not shake that "Preston School of Scandal" reputation that started so long ago. If those walls could talk, I am sure we would not be happy to hear what they had to say. There had been so much pain and so much death that could have been prevented.

If you ever have the chance to visit Ione, California and see Preston Castle for yourself, please take a tour. They are open every 1st and 3rd Saturdays of the month. Even if you just decide to drive by the "Castle" on a trip to Ione, please think of all that transpired there. Remember the good intentions that Superintendent Bank had from the start.

Now we know of the many bad things occurred that have long since been covered up. Let's also think of the positive stories of the few wards who left there and made a better life for themselves. I have heard the saying 'The road to hell is paved with good intentions'*, and perhaps it is true. Preston Castle must have been a hell of sorts, to many of those poor boys who suffered at the hands of wicked and cruel authorities there. Sadly, some of those boys never made it out.

---

* I chose this phrase because in society, it is commonly understood to mean that good intentions may not result in a good outcome due to unforeseen circumstances.

My heart goes out to all the boys who were mistreated and in some cases murdered, all whom were affected by that school, staff members such as Anna Corbin who died there, and the family members left to grieve their losses as well.

Let us remember the history of Preston and also those who have passed away in death here at this property. Let us never forget their stories, good or bad. Let us keep the history of Preston Castle alive for many more generations to come!

Sources & Bibliography:

Lafferty, John F., *The Preston School of Industry: A Centennial History 1894-1994 (1st Edition)*
People of the State of California vs Eugene Monroe, Case No. 5293, 1950
Willis, William L., *History of Sacramento County, California*, 1913.
Amador County History, Amador County Library
Various News Clippings & Photos, California State Archives
Preston School of Industry, Biennial Reports
Record Union, 2/26/1894
San Francisco Call, 4/5/1895
San Francisco Examiner, 4/6/1895
San Francisco Call, 11/1895
San Francisco Call, 11/17/1895
San Francisco Call, 3/16/1896
San Francisco Call, 5/16/1897
Statement of E.M. Preston, 5/16/1897
Statement of E.M. Preston, 5/16/1897
Affidavit filed with the Governor, E.E. Endicott, M.D., 11/14/1897
Los Angeles Times, 11/17/1897
Record Union, 11/17/1897
San Francisco Call, 11/17/1897
Affidavit filed with the Governor, H.R. Bernhard, 11/18/1897
San Francisco Call, 11/28/1897
Los Angeles Times, 11/28/1897
Los Angeles Times, 12/4/1897
San Francisco Call, 12/18/1897
San Francisco Call, 7/30/1899
San Francisco Call, 12/19/1900
Federal Census, 1900
Amador Ledger, 11/20/1903
San Francisco Call, 3/22/1904
San Francisco Call, 10/17/1911
San Francisco Call, 10/19/1911

San Francisco Call, 10/24/1911
San Francisco Call, 10/27/1911
Lodi Sentinel, 12/12/1916
Connelley, William., *A Standard History of Kansas and Kansans*,1918.
Ione Valley Echo, 4/1919
Amador Ledger, 4/21/1919
Letter from Preston School of Industry, Superintendent O.H. Close to State Board of Charities & Corrections, 4/4/1923
San Francisco Daily News, 7/10/1923
San Francisco Daily News, 7/16/1923
Evening Independent, 12/24/1923
Los Angeles Times, 8/8/1927
Federal Census, 1930
Ellensburg Daily, 9/6/1934
Lodi News, 1/2/1935
U.S. Military Enlistment Records, 1941
San Jose News, 4/27/1946
Lodi News Sentinel, 7/24/1946
Lodi News Sentinel, 5/3/1949
Oakland Tribune, 2/24/1950
Amador Ledger, 2/24/1950
Stockton Record, 2/27/1950
Oakland Tribune, 4/16/1950
Oakland Tribune, 4/27/1950
The Crisis, Magazine, June-1950
Lodi News Sentinel, 7/17/1950
Lodi News Sentinel, 4/9/1951
Youngstown Vindicator, 6/25/1951
Altus Times Democrat, 6/28/1951
Altus Times Democrat, 6/29/1951
Modesto Bee, 7/26/1951
Spokane Daily Chronicle, 7/27/1951
Telegraph Herald, 7/29/1951
News and Courier, 9/16/1951

St. Joseph News Press, 4/11/1952

Lodi News Sentinel, 7/19/1952

Modesto Bee, 5/15/1954

Shurtleff, William & Lawton, *Shurtleff & Lawton Family Genealogy*, 1994,1998, 2005

Rodriguez, Art, *East Side Dreams*, 1999

"*57 Year old Slaying Leaves Dark Memories in Preston Castle*"- Amador Ledger Dispatch, 10/27/2007- Reporter, Scott Thomas Anderson

Additional information obtained via Scott Thomas Anderson, Author & Crime Reporter, 2012

"*Goodbye Preston*", Center on Juvenile & Criminal Justice Website, contributor: Selene Teji, 6/10/2011

Oklahoma Department of Corrections, via Kevin Moore, 9/2012

Robert E. Byrd family history, Randolph Byrd, 10/3/2012

Photo Credits:

Photos from Preston School of Industry -Archived, pages 17, 50,

Sketch of Preston Castle by famous American writer/poet Joaquin Miller via 'San Francisco Call', 1895, page 10

Spreckels' Mansion, postcard, page 12

Photos from 'San Francisco Call' Newspaper clippings, pages 14, 15, 33, 35

Amador Ledger, page 42

Photos of Anna Corbin, Oakland Tribune, 2/24/1950, page 76

Anna Corbin, State Archives, page 60

San Francisco Daily News, page 48

Photo of Eugene Monroe, Modesto Bee, 7/26/1951, page 69

Cover Photo by Jay Silva

Photo (view from turret) by Jay Silva, page 13

Back Cover Photo by Roland Boulware

Photos by Roland Boulware, pages 83

Photos by J'aime Rubio, pages 8, 13, 37, 47, 60, 86

Photo by Sandy Montanez, page 77

Photos of Robert E. Byrd, c/o Randolph Byrd, page 29

Photo of Art Rodriguez, c/o Tita Rodriguez Para, pages 79, 82

Photo from Loren Bender, findagrave.com, page 63

Photo from the Preston Review Newspaper (defunct), 55

Made in the USA
Las Vegas, NV
10 June 2021